How to Receive the Holy Spirit

David Littlewood

Trywalla Publications

Copyright © 2014 David Littlewood

All rights reserved.
No parts of this publication may be reproduced or transmitted in any form or by any means, mechanical, electronic, photocopying or otherwise, without the prior written consent of the author.

Short extracts may be used for review purposes.

ISBN
978-0-9928429-3-2

Trywalla Publications
trywalla@gmail.com

Contents

Preface	5
Introduction	9
1. A Personal Experience	13
2. The Promise	23
3. The Importance	27
4. What happens when we receive?	31
5. Speaking in Tongues	43
6. Hindrances to receiving	55
7. How do we receive the Holy Spirit?	61
8, A Prayer for the Holy Spirit	69
A Final Word	71

Preface

It had been a thrilling evening. The church I was speaking at was having some special meetings on the Holy Spirit and I had just given a talk on what is generally known as the 'Baptism in the Spirit'. When I gave the appeal, quite a few people had come to the front of the church to be prayed for.

As we prayed, people began receiving the Holy Spirit, speaking fluently in other tongues just like Jesus' first disciples did on the first Day of Pentecost.

One gentleman on the end of the row was really having a great time. His face was radiant as he stood praising the Lord in a language he'd never learned. When I talked with him after the meeting he told me he was a recent convert and that was the first time he'd ever spoken in tongues. He then added, with a look of sheer joy on his face: "I've just walked up to the cash machine to get some money for the bookstall. I spoke in tongues all the way there and all the way back!"

It struck me then, as it has on a number of other occasions, just how easy it is for people to receive the Holy Spirit, once they are given a few simple instructions. One problem is we so often try to complicate something that God wants to be very simple. The Holy Spirit is a gift from God and all we have to do to receive a gift just to take it.

My grandchildren are great ones at receiving gifts. When I say, "Grandpa's got a present for you," they don't try and complicate matters by asking me what they must do to receive their gift. They just grab it!

The Bible tells us that God is our Father and he gives good gifts to his children. He doesn't expect us to earn his gifts or even do anything in return for them. All he wants us to do is to 'grab' them from him. In fact, Strong's Concordance tells us that the Greek word the New Testament uses for 'receive' - *lambano* - has the sense of 'to lay hold by *aggressively (actively) accepting* what is available'. In other words, it means 'to grab hold of'.

Now to those of us brought up properly, the thought of 'grabbing' a gift does not seem very polite. But God does not want us to be polite, he wants us to be empowered by receiving the gift of his Holy Spirit. And, just like little children, he wants us to eagerly 'grab hold' of the gift he gives us.

In writing this book I am responding to a number of requests to put down in written form the talk I have given many times on receiving the Baptism in the Holy Spirit. In the years since the beginnings of the Pentecostal Movement a huge number of books have been written around this subject and, as many contain excellent teaching, I have not tried to add to them. The purpose of this book is rather to give people a few guidelines as to how, in practical terms, they can receive or 'grab hold' of the gift of God.

How to Receive the Holy Spirit

Introduction

Hundreds of years before Christ came to the earth, God gave a remarkable promise to a prophet named Joel. There will come a time, God said, "when I will pour out my Spirit on all people. Your sons and daughters will prophesy, your old men will dream dreams and your young men will see visions. In fact I will pour out my Spirit in those days on all my servants, both men and women." (Joel 2:28-29) He also added that in the so-called 'last days' that "everyone who calls on the name of the Lord will be saved." (Joel 2:32)

To pious Jews of Joel's day, the thought of God's Spirit being poured out upon all people of every race must have been revolutionary. After all, to them, Israel were the only people on earth God had chosen to deal with. And even within the nation of Israel, experiences of the Holy Spirit tended to be few and far between, usually confined to special servants of God like prophets and kings. The thought that there would come a day when ordinary servants of God would receive vital and personal experiences of the Holy Spirit would have been amazing. And as for people outside of Israel -

the so-called Gentile nations - receiving the Holy Spirit, that was unthinkable!

Yet all over the world today, the promise given to an obscure Israelite prophet is coming to pass. God is pouring out his Spirit in an unprecedented way on all people, regardless of race, colour or gender. Even countries that have been notoriously difficult to reach with the gospel are seeing remarkable church growth, with thousands coming to Christ and huge churches being established. In fact, it can be safely said that today the true church is growing faster than at any time in its history.

One significant factor in this growth has been the rediscovery of what it means for ordinary Christians to be filled with the Holy Spirit. Throughout the centuries God has given great ministry gifts to his church. People like George Whitefield, John Wesley, D L Moody, Charles Finney, Billy Graham and many other highly gifted men have done extraordinary work in preaching the gospel and promoting revival. But the secret of the growth of the early church appears to lie in ordinary Christians, filled with the Holy Spirit, sharing the gospel in the power of the Spirit.

Around the beginning of the 20th century, God's people began once again to experience what both John the Baptist and Jesus described as the 'Baptism in the Holy Spirit'. What's more, when they received this experience, they began to speak in other tongues as the Holy Spirit enabled them, just like those those first disciples did on the day of Pentecost.

For these people - many of them simple, uneducated believers - this experience was the rediscovery of vital New Testament Christianity. Not only did they preach the new birth, but they also expected the signs and wonders found in the New Testament - healing, miracles, prophecy and other miraculous gifts - to follow their preaching.

Sadly, many of these people were marginalised by the church in general. They went on to form the so-called 'Pentecostal Movement', keeping the experience of the Baptism in the Spirit alive in their teaching and practice. However, during the 1960s came a breakthrough when people of all church denominations began receiving this experience. Since then receiving the Baptism in the Holy Spirit accompanied by speaking in other tongues has become a common experience among Bible believing Christians.

Yet throughout my ministry I have met many people, even in churches which are sympathetic to Charismatic / Pentecostal experience, who have yet to receive what God has promised them. The problem is often that they don't know exactly how to take hold of God's gift. This book aims to provide teaching on the subject of the Baptism in the Spirit along with some practical guidance on how we can receive the gift of God that empowers us for living in a New Testament lifestyle.

One problem we often have as Christians is that we try and complicate what God intends to be simple and straightforward. Over many years of ministry I have found that there is nothing complicated about receiving the gift of the Holy Spirit. It is my prayer that this book will prove helpful to God's people as they seek to live out their lives in the turbulent and momentous days in which we live.

1
A Personal Experience

In 1966 I went to the University of Essex near Colchester, UK, to study science. I eventually graduated with a good honours degree in physics, but during my first year at university I gained something far greater than any earthly degree - I found Jesus Christ as my Saviour. Despite the university at the time being a hotbed of left wing activism, I managed to fall in with a group of Christians who invited me to attend a Bible study group.

I'd gone to university a nominal believer whose Christianity extended to attending church once a week and trying not to swear on a Sunday. However, largely due to the infinite patience of the rest of the Bible study group (who put up with my endless arguments with great fortitude) I became convinced there was a lot more to the Christian faith than I had gleaned from the rather insipid brand of Christianity I had encountered up till then. It dawned on my somewhat slow spiritual understanding that these people had something that I, for all my smart 'intellectual' arguments, simply did not have - a real relationship with God.

A few weeks into the Bible studies, the leader of the university Christian Union - a young man called Mike - invited me to attend a house party was being held at the seaside resort of Cromer. I agreed to come, although I arrogantly added to my acceptance of the kind invitation that, "I probably won't agree with anything anyone says!" Mike graciously assured me that no-one would mind and seemed pleased as he added my name to the list. I didn't realise at the time that God was setting a trap for me!

The house party was held at a Christian Endeavour holiday home, a redoubtable establishment with a rather eccentric landlady who sat on the stairs as we went to bed pointing girls in one direction and boys in the other. I thought all this very quaint but was really impressed with the speaker we had for the weekend. He was a young man, 'Dickie' Dowsett, who was acting as a travelling secretary for the then Inter-Varsity Fellowship, an evangelical organisation devoted to spreading the gospel of Christ in universities and colleges of higher education. Dickie took as his theme for the weekend, 'Jesus, the Way, the Truth and the Life'. I don't remember an awful lot of what he said but the word of God was obviously making an impression on my rebellious heart and know-all mind.

One of the hymns we sang on the Saturday evening was Charles Wesley's great gospel hymn, 'And Can it Be'. One line that stuck with me and kept going around in my mind after I'd gone to bed was when Wesley declares in the words of his own testimony:

My chains fell off, my heart was free,
I rose went forth and followed Thee.

Although I did not know it at the time, it was the Holy Spirit calling me to come to Christ. I responded, and on 13th November 1966, lying in a somewhat uncomfortable bed in the Christian Endeavour holiday home in Cromer, I gave my life to Jesus Christ. I went to bed a sinner with no relationship with God; I came down in the morning a new creation in Christ. As the old hymn says, "O Happy Day!"

The effect of my newfound faith was pretty dramatic; the first time I picked up a Bible it was obvious to me that something had changed. Whereas before I had read the Bible with very little understanding, it now appeared a living book to me. The words almost seemed to move on the page! I realise now that it was because the Holy Spirit had made my own (human) spirit born-again, giving me understanding into the words he had inspired nearly 2,000 years before. I became really eager to fellowship with other believers to discuss my new found faith and I undoubtedly pestered my Christian friends no end into spending time which they should have been spending on their studies answering my questions! Churchgoing was still a bit of a chore but that was to change during the next university term.

I came back home for the Christmas holidays with a book I purchased from the Christian Union bookstall. It was called *The Cross and the Switchblade* and recounted the story of a young minister, David Wilkerson, and his mission among violent gangs of New York. The book had become a sensational best seller with its depiction of the vibrant type of New Testament Christianity that changes hardened criminals into fervent witnesses for Christ. I was thrilled that this kind of Christianity still existed - I thought till then it was strictly confined to the pages of the New Testament.

I was particularly struck with an experience that Wilkerson called the 'Baptism in the Holy Spirit' which he said was accompanied by speaking in other tongues as the Holy Spirit supernaturally gave the person power to do so. Although many of my Christian friends cautioned me against seeking such an experience, saying that such things are not for today or that we shouldn't seek experiences like this for the sake of it, I was now filled with a desire for something more than the sincere yet seemingly powerless Christianity that had been my experience up till then.

Opportunity came when the local Pentecostal minister, David Petts, was invited to give a talk one Saturday evening at the Christian Union. Providentially, his church - which was just a tin hut with the label 'Full Gospel Mission' on the notice board - was right opposite the bed and breakfast where I was staying as a student in Colchester. David (who would later become the principal of the Assemblies of God Bible College and a leading figure in the worldwide Pentecostal movement) gave his talk on Romans 12:1 to the small group of students who gathered in a bedsit where the meeting was held. I was immediately struck by the power and authority of his preaching and after the meeting could not wait to talk to him about the Baptism in the Spirit and speaking in tongues. He dealt with my impulsiveness very graciously and invited me, if I was interested, to attend his church the next morning.

The next morning I made the short journey from my student digs to the tin hut across the road. To my surprise I found it was filled with people, younger as well as older. The service amazed me - it seemed to me so spontaneous compared with the formality I had been used to. There were also evidences of the supernatural, with messages in tongues, prophecies and prayer for healing. I was so fascinated by the service and the welcome I received, that I returned for the evening meeting. Providentially, David Petts had chosen as his subject the Baptism in the Spirit and the difference it makes to people's lives today.

I sat there drinking in his teaching and at the end of the meeting when he asked if anyone wanted to be prayed for in order to receive the

Baptism in the Holy Spirit, my hand went straight in the air even though I was totally unused to responding to public appeals. Actually, I was so eager to receive this experience that I think if the preacher had asked me to come to the front and stand on my head I would have done that as well!

After the meeting David Petts took me back to his home so that we could iron out a few questions that were buzzing around in my mind. He then asked me if I'd like him to pray for me. Having received my reply in the affirmative, David put his hands on me and prayed that I would receive the Holy Spirit. I drank in the power of God and within half a minute was praising God and in other tongues. Having left David and his wife to a well earned night's sleep I walked back to my student digs speaking in tongues all the way.

The experience I received that night opened up a whole new world of supernatural Christianity to me. Not only did Jesus become far more real to me but now I had the possibility of exercising the gifts of the Spirit through the power of God that had come to dwell within me. Above all I was able to witness to those around me with a far greater degree of assurance of the certainty of my faith. As Jesus said, "You shall receive power when the Holy Spirit is come upon you and you shall be my witnesses.................. to the ends of the earth." (Acts 1:8)

To my great joy, quite a number of my friends in the university Christian Union, having heard me talk about my experience, themselves received the Baptism in the Spirit and spoke in tongues. We certainly had some memorable times seeking God together. I particularly remember one prayer meeting we had we started (student style) at 10 o'clock at night and didn't finish until one o'clock in the morning. We were so caught up in the Holy Spirit that no one had noticed the time. It was my first experience (one of many I am pleased to say) of what the Bible calls 'praying in the Holy Spirit'.

Having left university I taught physics for 11 years before answering a call to the Christian ministry. One of the greatest joys in my ministry has been leading people into the Baptism in the Holy Spirit. By the grace of God I have seen many people in different parts of the world filled with the Holy Spirit.

After one such meeting in Africa where a whole line of people, one after the other, started to speak in tongues, someone remarked to me, "You make it so simple!" That to me is the secret of receiving the Holy Spirit - it is all very simple – as simple as receiving a birthday present or drinking a glass of water. The problem is many Christians, through a lack of understanding, try to make things very complicated. But receiving from God is actually very easy because he wants to give good gifts to his children.

When the Welsh revival happened in 1904, many people visited the places where the Spirit was being out poured with such power. One of them said, "I have come to find out the secret of your revival," to which revival leader Evan Roberts replied, "There is no secret, brother! Just ask and receive!" Similarly we could say there is no secret in receiving the Baptism in the Holy Spirit - just ask and receive!

It is my prayer that as people read the principles set out in this little book, they will come to an understanding of how the Holy Spirit is received today. As Peter said in his sermon on that first day of Pentecost: "This promise is for you, and your children, and for all who are far off – for all whom the Lord our God shall call!" (Acts 2:39)

2
The Promise

During the last meal he shared with his disciples before he went to the cross, Jesus gave them the promise that he would send someone whom he called "another Helper" (John 14:16) to them. He promised them that having this Helper around would be just like having him around. He promised his disciples, "I will not leave you as orphans, I will come to you." (John 14:18)

Now in Jewish life in those days it was customary for a Jewish rabbi or teacher to gather round him a group of disciples whom he would instruct. The relationship was so strong that if the rabbi died, the disciples would be known as 'orphans'. Now Jesus knew then that in a few hours he was going to be taken away to die on a cross, leaving his despairing disciples (apparently) as 'orphans'. However, he also knew that through the power of God he would rise from the dead. He would then appear to those same disciples in his resurrected body and finally ascend to heaven from where he would send the Holy Spirit - the 'Helper' he was talking about.

By the aid of this 'Helper' the disciples would be able to do all the things that they had seen Jesus do during his ministry on earth. In fact Jesus (John 14:12) said that by the power of the Holy Spirit, the disciples would be even able to do greater 'works'- ie miracles – than he had done!

Even more important than the miracles was the fact that the person of the Holy Spirit would be with the disciples wherever they went. That is why Jesus said that it was better for the disciples if he went away (John 16:7) because then he could send the Holy Spirit to them. When Jesus was present in his body on earth, things were absolutely wonderful wherever he was. But, of course, because he was confined to a body he could only be in one place at one time. If he was in Galilee then he couldn't be in Jerusalem; if he was with one group of disciples he couldn't be with the rest. But now, through the Holy Spirit, he could be with all his disciples all the time. What's more, they themselves would carry the Holy Spirit around with them, giving them access to the Spirit's power wherever they went. As Jesus said to them, "he [the Holy Spirit] lives with you now and later will be in you." (John 14:17)

How to Receive the Holy Spirit

The amazing fact is that when someone becomes a Christian the Holy Spirit comes to live in them. Paul teaches us that we who were once 'dead' in sin become 'alive' to God through the work of the Holy Spirit (Ephesians 2:5). We are made 'new creatures' in Christ Jesus (2 Corinthians 5:17).

But God does not want us to stop there. He also wants us to do the things Christ did by filling us with the miraculous power of the Holy Spirit. He told his disciples that they would receive power when the Holy Spirit came upon them and that they would be his witnesses to the ends of the earth. (Acts 1:8) It was through the power of God given to them by the Holy Spirit that these few men and women, who the Jewish authorities despised as "ignorant and unlearned", managed to turn not only Jerusalem but the whole world upside down with their proclamation of the good news of Jesus.

How to Receive the Holy Spirit

3
The Importance

After rising from the dead Jesus spent 40 days with his disciples teaching them about the new Kingdom that they were about to proclaim to the world. Most of what he said is not recorded, but Luke tells us that Jesus told his disciples that they were to wait for the Holy Spirit before they began their mission. On one occasion he said: "I am going to send you what my Father has promised; but stay in the city until you have been clothed with power from on high." (Luke 24:49)

Later, when the disciples asked him questions about how he was going to establish the new Kingdom he had promised he told them: "But you will receive power when the Holy Spirit comes upon you; and you will be my witnesses in Jerusalem, and in all Judaea and Samaria, and to the ends of the earth. (Acts 1:8)

We can see just from these two quotes just how important it was that the disciples received the power of the Holy Spirit before they began their mission. Indeed, without the Holy Spirit their chances of success were less than negligible. After all, they were just a motley bunch of fishermen, tax collectors, zealots and other society outcasts who had gathered round Jesus. To pit them against the power of the religious Jewish establishment (which had managed to persuade the unwilling Roman governor to execute Jesus himself) and the merciless might of the Roman Empire (which had carried out the execution) would have appeared the greatest mismatch in history.

Yet within a generation, in spite of horrendous persecution, the good news of Jesus Christ had spread throughout the Roman Empire. What had enabled the simple and unlearned disciples of Jesus to succeed against such incredible odds? Nothing less than the power of the Holy Spirit sent from the Father by Jesus on the first day of Pentecost.

As disciples of Jesus today we are also called to be witnesses to the generation in which we live. But we need to learn we cannot do it on our own. Sadly, one of the greatest mistakes of the Church throughout the ages has been to neglect the work of the Holy Spirit and to rely on human cleverness or ability. That has always been a recipe for spiritual death and numerical decline. But where the church has experienced the power of the Holy Spirit working among believers, its growth has often been extraordinary, even in places which have traditionally been resistant to Christian evangelism.

One example of this is the church in China. When the missionaries departed just after the war, it was feared that the Chinese church would die. Yet in spite of savage persecution by a hostile regime, the church in China has experienced the most extraordinary growth. What has made the difference? The power of the Holy Spirit working among believers.

And what about us as believers in our increasingly secularised Western culture? How can we make an impact on the society in which we live - a society which since the 'Swinging 60s' has been rapidly departing from the Judaeo-Christian values on which it was built? Countless plans – many of them good ones – have been thought up by innovative and dedicated church leaders, but they appear to have made little impact in arresting the decline of Western Christendom. What is needed in these desperate circumstances is nothing less than the same power of God that worked in those first believers in the early church.

How to Receive the Holy Spirit

The good news is that power is available to believers today through the Baptism in the Holy Spirit. It is this power that will enable us not only to stand as individual believers but also to make a difference to the society around us, in our homes, in our neighbourhoods and at the places where we work. The promise of God to us is that when we are filled with the Holy Spirit we are given power to take the person of the risen Christ with us wherever we go.

4
What happens when we receive the Holy Spirit?

There are five clear instances in Luke's history of the Acts of the Apostles where believers receive the Holy Spirit. Let's have a look at them to see whether there are some common factors in the experiences:

1. On the Day of Pentecost (Acts 2)

Luke tells us that Jesus' disciples were met together waiting for the Holy Spirit that Jesus had promised them they would receive before beginning their mission of preaching the gospel to the ends of the earth. As they waited, "Suddenly a sound like the blowing of a violent wind came from heaven and filled the whole house where they were sitting. They saw what seemed to be tongues of fire that separated and came to rest on each of them. All of them were filled with the Holy Spirit and began to speak in other tongues as the Spirit enabled them." (Acts 2:2-4)

From this we see that when these disciples were filled with the Holy Spirit they began to speak in other tongues as the Holy Spirit enabled them, much to the amazement of the crowd that gathered. These Jewish pilgrims, who had gathered in Jerusalem from all over the then known world, heard these Galileans telling the wonderful works of God in their own native languages. Speaking in tongues was actually the first miraculous event that happened in the early church. It appears to have been so convincing a miracle that over 3000 people turned to the brand-new Christian faith after hearing Peter's explanation!

2. In Samaria (Acts 8)

Despite the impact the gospel of Jesus Christ made in Jerusalem, the Jewish authorities were not impressed and persecution against the Church soon arose against what was considered a heretical sect. Not only were the apostles, Peter and John, arrested and beaten, but before long a brilliant young preacher called Stephen so offended the establishment that he was set upon by a lynch mob and stoned to death. This was the start of an intense persecution led by a young Jewish zealot named Saul. To escape the persecution many of the disciples had to flee Jerusalem.

In the providence of God, this terrible time was extremely beneficial for the growth of the church, as the scattered disciples took the gospel with them wherever they went. One such person was Philip, who sought refuge in nearby Samaria. A gifted evangelist, he preached the gospel with great power to the Samaritans. When they saw the miracles of healing and deliverance that happened in the name of Jesus, many of the local people turned to Christ.

Philip then sent for the apostles, Peter and John, to come and establish these new Christians in the faith – and especially to pray for them that they might receive the Holy Spirit.

When Peter and John arrived, Luke tells us that they placed their hands on the new believers who immediately received the Holy Spirit (Acts 8:17). Now although it doesn't mention any specific sign that happened, Luke's narrative implies that something wonderful and miraculous took place. In fact, he tells us that a local sorcerer named Simon was so impressed with the supernatural nature of what happened that he offered the disciples money in order that he might be able to impart the experience to others. Of course, Peter soundly rebuked him for making such a wicked suggestion; but the very fact that good money was offered does illustrate that something miraculous was happening. After all, as a sorcerer, Simon would have made his living by supernatural manifestations (whether real or bogus) and now wanted to get in on the act on something he knew was quite remarkable.

In his commentary on Acts, F F Bruce says that the external signs that accompanied the reception of the Holy Spirit by the Samaritans were "of so impressive a nature that Simon Magus craved the power to reproduce them at will."[1] Looking at this passage in the context of other scriptures, I have little doubt that what attracted the sorcerer's attention was the fact that when these new converts received the Holy Spirit, it was attended by the same external manifestation as had marked the Spirit's descent on the day of Pentecost – ie speaking in other tongues.

---

[1] Bruce F F *The Book of Acts* (Marshall, Morgan and Scott) p.183

3. Paul (Acts 9)

In Acts 9 we see the young Pharisee, Saul of Tarsus, heading up a massive persecution against what he felt was a total aberration of the Jewish faith. These followers of Jesus of Nazareth, he reckoned, were violating the law of God. This heresy had therefore to be stamped out before it had a chance to take root and corrupt the faith that had been his life since childhood.

Saul was on his way to Damascus when an incredible event happened. None other than the risen Jesus of Nazareth, whose followers the young zealot was about to have rounded up and imprisoned, appeared to him. The vision was so bright that Saul was blinded and had to be led into Damascus where he stayed in a house on Straight Street. There he prayed and fasted, seeking to get things right with the Jesus he had been persecuting.

Meanwhile God had spoken to a faithful disciple named Ananias and told him to go and visit Saul. Although Ananias was reluctant to go and see the man who was leading the opposition to his faith, he obeyed God and when he arrived at the house where Saul was staying, he found the man of Tarsus repentant and ready to be baptised.

Now it is useful to note Ananias' words to the still blind Saul. After placing his hands on him he said: "Brother Saul, the Lord—Jesus, who appeared to you on the road as you were coming here—has sent me so that you may see again and be filled with the Holy Spirit." (Acts 9:17) The first priority for this new convert after regaining his sight would be to receive the Holy Spirit.

Luke then tells us that the future apostle was miraculously healed of his blindness and was baptised. From what has been inferred before we might also assume that he was baptised in the Holy Spirit as well as being immersed in water. The early church certainly believed that baptism in water and baptism in the Holy Spirit were two parts of the same experience of 'one baptism' (Ephesians 4:5). Hence the first experience that the future apostle Paul would have had after his conversion would have been his baptism – in water and in the Spirit.

But would Paul have spoken in tongues when Ananias laid his hands on him for him to receive the Holy Spirit? I think it is very likely as later, in a letter to the Corinthians, Paul tells them: "I thank God I speak in tongues more than you all." (1 Cor 14:18) The most logical place for him to have received this ability to speak in tongues so fluently was when he was baptised in the Holy Spirit.

In addition, in his later ministry, Paul obviously expected people to speak in tongues when they received the Holy Spirit. Hence when in Acts 19 he asks a group of disciples at Ephesus, "Did you receive the Holy Spirit when you believed?" the question implies a definite, recognisable experience. A few verses later, when the Ephesians receive this experience at the hands of Paul, they speak in tongues.

Putting these facts together, one might assume that it would have been remarkable if Paul's initial experience of the Holy Spirit had not included speaking in tongues.

4. Cornelius and his household (Acts 10)

Following the conversion of Saul of Tarsus the Church enjoyed a time of relative peace. However, the faith was still confined to those within the Jewish race. To strict and pious Jews it was unthinkable that the heathen Gentiles should share in the grace of God. However, God was about to intervene in the shape of a Roman centurion called Cornelius who lived at Caesarea.

Cornelius was a 'God-fearer' - a Gentile who worshipped the God of the Jews. As he was praying one day he received a vision from God telling him to send for a man called Peter. At the same time the apostle Peter also received a vision of animals crawling around in a sheet. They were animals that the Jewish faith regarded as unclean. When a voice from heaven told Peter to "kill and eat" he told God that he had never eaten anything unclean or common. A voice then told him: "What God has cleansed you must not call common!" (Acts 10:15)

Peter was puzzled about this vision until men arrived from Cornelius asking him to visit his house. When he reached the house of

Cornelius Peter then did the unthinkable. Bearing in mind what God had told him in the vision, he went into the house of a Gentile - a man considered 'unclean' by the Jewish law.

When he heard about the vision Cornelius had received, Peter preached to the centurion and to his gathered household the good news about Jesus. Before he even got to the end of his sermon, the Bible says that the Holy Spirit descended on everyone who was there. Peter and the Jews who were with him were astonished because they realised that these Gentiles had received the Holy Spirit.

How did Peter know that Cornelius and his family had received the Holy Spirit? Luke says that "they heard them speaking with tongues and praising God." (Acts 10:46) Later, when relating the story to his fellow Jewish believers, Peter tells them how the Holy Spirit had fallen on these Gentiles just like he had done upon the Jews on the day of Pentecost with exactly the same sign - speaking in other tongues.

5. The Christians at Ephesus (Acts 19)

We have already seen that some time during his remarkable ministry, the apostle Paul visited the city of Ephesus, the site of which is now in modern day Turkey. There he found a small group of about a dozen believers. Significantly, the first question Paul asked them was, "did you receive the Holy Spirit when you believed?" (Acts 19:2)

On hearing that these believers had not even heard of the Holy Spirit, Paul then examined them a little more closely and found that they needed some better instruction in the fundamentals of the Christian faith. Having completed a brief introductory course for new believers, Paul first baptised them in water, and then laid his hands on them that they might receive the Holy Spirit. When he did this, Luke tells us that, "the Holy Spirit came upon them, and they began speaking in tongues and prophesying." (Acts 19:6)

So what might we expect to see when people receive the Holy Spirit? From the above cases which are outlined by Luke in the Acts of the Apostles, we see that the manifestations include tongues, praise and prophecy. The common thread that runs through all these experiences is speaking in tongues. Hence, although there is no absolute statement in Scripture to the effect, we can infer from what is recorded in the Acts of the Apostles and elsewhere that when people are baptised in the Holy Spirit, they speak in tongues.

How to Receive the Holy Spirit

5
Speaking in Tongues

What is tongues?

'Tongues' is speaking in a language that has never been learned by the power of the Holy Spirit. When someone is filled with the Holy Spirit tongues are given them as a sign of this experience.

Sometimes the tongues might be recognised by someone who happens to know the language that is spoken. On a missions trip to Africa with some other English ministers, we prayed for some of the African pastors to receive the Holy Spirit. To our surprise, one of them began praising God in English even though it was quite obvious he didn't know the language.

When the language is recognised (as on the Day of Pentecost), tongues can be a 'sign' to those who are not yet believers. During a meeting held by the American evangelist, Maria Woodworth-Etter, a man gave a long utterance in other tongues, after which a Jewish rabbi stood up and told the astonished congregation that the man had been telling him about Jesus in fluent Hebrew!

Of course, these cases are exceptional, as they indeed were in the Acts of the Apostles. In most cases when people speak in other tongues, the languages are not recognised. Yet this does not diminish the wonder of communicating in this way to the living God.

What is the point of speaking with tongues?

When I was seeking the Baptism in the Spirit, sincere but cautious Christian friends warned me not to seek 'experience'. Tongues, they told me, is the 'least' of the gifts of the Spirit. In fact, they said, the apostle Paul himself spoke against the use of tongues; he taught that love was the greatest of the 'gifts' and we should seek that instead.

Such misguided thinking neglects the fact that Paul, in his letter to the Corinthians, tells his readers that, "I thank God that I speak in tongues more than any of you!" (1 Corinthians 14:18) The fact is that, when writing to the Corinthians, Paul was not despising what he knew was a remarkable and useful gift of God. Rather he was cautioning them against the misuse of the gift of tongues in a public meeting. In their enthusiasm the immature

Corinthian congregation had allowed the public use of tongues to get out of hand!

Even so, Paul's solution is not to denigrate tongues, let alone discourage the use of them. As with all public manifestations, he teaches, that the use of spiritual gifts should be orderly and done for the benefit of other members of the congregation, not self-aggrandisement. Then follows the famous chapter, 1 Corinthians 13, in which Paul extols love, not as a spiritual gift but as a way to follow when using spiritual gifts. Nowhere does Paul tell us to seek love *instead* of spiritual gifts. Rather he sums it up that we are to follow the *way* of love while *eagerly desiring* the gifts of the Spirit. (1 Cor 14:1) After all, even if tongues is the 'least' of the gifts, as it is the gift of God himself it is surely worth having!

Paul may have put certain restrictions on the public use of tongues, but there are certainly none when we use tongues in private. As we have already seen, Paul thanks God for his ability to speak in tongues more than anyone. It is therefore quite obvious that speaking in tongues was a large part of his own private devotional life.

So why is it helpful for us to speak in tongues? There are actually quite a few reasons but for the purpose of this study we shall just deal with five.

First, **speaking in tongues brings an increased intimacy with God in prayer**. Paul tells us that: "When I speak in tongues my spirit prays but my mind is unfruitful." Now sometimes it is a very good thing for our minds to be unfruitful as when we come to God our minds can be full of other things. I know when I begin praying my mind is often full of things which I have to do during the day which may be a distraction from my fellowship with God.

However, if we begin to speak in tongues our spirit starts to pray. We know we are praying aright because it is God who is directing our prayers through the tongues we are uttering. As we continue to speak in tongues our minds start to focus on God and we then have a wonderful lead-in as we start to pray in our normal language. As Paul says: "I will pray with my spirit [ie in tongues], but I will also pray with my understanding." (1 Corinthians 14:15) So as a lead-in to our prayer, or when we are finding prayer difficult, a time of speaking in tongues can bring us into the presence of God.

Second, **tongues can bring us a new power in prayer**. Through the gift of tongues we can pray in a whole new spiritual dimension. Paul tells us that sometimes we do not know how we ought to pray but it is at these times that the Holy Spirit can intercede for us "with groanings too deep for words." He continues: "And he who searches hearts knows what is the mind of the Spirit, because the Spirit intercedes for the saints according to the will of God." (Rom 8:26-27 ASV)

Although these "groanings" which are "[otherwise] inexpressible" or "too deep for [human] words [alone]," may not exclusively refer to speaking tongues, it does not seem an unreasonable assumption that Paul would have expected that tongues form at least part of the prayers that we cannot otherwise express as the Spirit "intercedes" through us.

The same thing may be said of Paul's exhortation to the Ephesians to be "praying always with all prayer and supplication in the Spirit." (Eph 5:18) Although, again, this probably does not refer exclusively to speaking in tongues, certainly tongues will play a big part of our prayer lives as we pray "in the Spirit."

Praying in tongues can be tremendously liberating as we can intercede for things we know little or nothing about. And when we come to God with a burden, praying in tongues in faith can ensure our intercessions are entirely in accordance with the will of God. The British missionary, Jackie Pullinger, who has done an extraordinary work among drug addicts of Hong Kong, says she found a new dimension of prayer when she began to pray in tongues regularly. She describes this in chapter 5 of her book, 'Chasing the Dragon':

"Every day........I prayed in the language of the Spirit. Fifteen minutes by the clock. I still found it to be an exercise. Before praying in the Spirit I said, 'Lord, I don't know how to pray, or whom to pray for. Will you pray through me - and will you lead me to the people who want you.' And I would begin my fifteen minute stint.

"After about six weeks I noticed something remarkable. Those I talked to about Christ believed. I could not understand it at first and wondered how my Chinese had so suddenly improved, or if I had stumbled on a splendid new evangelistic technique. But I was saying the same things as before. It was some time before I realised what had changed. This time I was talking about Jesus to people who wanted to hear. I had let God have a hand in my prayers and it produced a direct result. Instead of my deciding what I wanted to do for God and asking his blessing I was asking him to do his will through me as I prayed in the language he gave me.

"Now I found that person after person wanted to receive Jesus. I could not be proud - I could only wonder that God let me be a small part of his work. And so the emotion came. It never came while I prayed, but when I saw the results of these prayers I was literally delighted."

One reason I believe the devil wants to discourage us from speaking in tongues regularly is that he knows the power in prayer released through them when we exercise this God-given gift!

Thirdly, **tongues bring a new dimension to our worship of God**. Paul tells the Corinthians that not only does he pray in tongues – he sings in tongues as well! He says: "I will sing [praise] with my spirit, but I will also sing with my understanding." (1 Cor 14:15) Hence, singing in other tongues made up part of the Apostle's worship to God.

When the disciples first received the Holy Spirit on the Day of Pentecost, the amazed crowd heard them speaking in other tongues and "declaring the wonderful works of God." (Acts 2:11) Therefore it appears that speaking in tongues presents us with a powerful tool to enhance our worship of God.

Our worship enters a new dimension when we speak or sing in tongues. Often, just like we don't know how to pray as we ought, so we cannot find the words to express our love and gratitude to God for all he has done for us. Moreover, we cannot find the words to express the excellence of his majesty and person.

This is where tongues – sung or spoken – can aid us in our worship. I heard the story of a young man who was praising God in a meeting. As he poured out his heart to God, he said the familiar words: "Lord, we worship you, we honour you, we adore you!" Then, being a sincere and thoughtful young man, he stopped and said, "No, Lord! I cannot find words to adore you!" He later found speaking in tongues a powerful means to express the adoration of his heart to God.

Fourthly, **tongues is a miraculous gateway to the gifts of the Holy Spirit**. In 1 Corinthians 12:7-11, Paul outlines the nine miraculous gifts of the Spirit. It is not the purpose of this booklet to go into them in detail; just to say that these gifts are entirely supernatural and work according to the will of the Holy Spirit through individuals in the church.

Although speaking in tongues is included among the gifts it may also be seen as the 'gateway' to the other gifts. Of course, as the Holy Spirit gives the gifts "as he wills" (1 Cor 12:11) there is no hard and fast rule. But in general people tend to manifest tongues before going on to use and enjoy the other miraculous gifts – including healing, prophecy, working of miracles, etc – that God has given to his church.

Fifthly **tongues are a means of 'charging ourselves up' spiritually**. Paul tells us that "he who speaks in an unknown tongue edifies himself" (1 Cor 14:4) The Greek word often translated 'edify' is *oikodomeo* which means 'to build up', as in building a house. Relating it to a familiar device of our own age, we can speculate it is the word that Paul might have used for charging a mobile phone, had (of course!) one been available to him in the first century.

We all know that when we use a mobile phone the battery runs down. Indeed, let it run down too far and it won't work. The solution is, of course, to plug it into an electricity supply and charge it up. Similarly, as believers working for Christ we are often in need of a spiritual 'recharge'. One simple way of recharging our 'spiritual batteries' is by taking time to speak in tongues. As we do so our spirit communicates with God and draws on the vast resources available to us.

Are you feeling in need of a 'spiritual recharge'? Use the gift of speaking in other tongues that God has given you for this purpose.

Hence we see that rather than being 'the least of the gifts' as some have supposed, speaking in tongues is a wonderful spiritual resource, readily available to us any time we care to use it. It can be used for our own benefit or the benefit of others. When we consider the vast spiritual armoury God has given us through this gift we see what the Apostle Paul meant when he said: "I thank God I speak in tongues more than you all!"

How to Receive the Holy Spirit

6
Hindrances to receiving

Although over the years I have seen literally hundreds of people receive the Holy Spirit in answer to prayer, with or without the laying of hands, there are still people who have difficulties with the sheer simplicity of how God gives the Holy Spirit. Ironically, these are often good, sincere Christian people who have been taught that they must do certain things to please God before he will give you the Holy Spirit. The fact is, however, that the Holy Spirit has already been given to all those who believe. And it is actually very easy to receive what God has already given! The problem is that so often we make things complicated when God has already laid out a simple solution.

If we look at what Jesus taught on receiving the Holy Spirit, he said: "So I say to you: Ask and it will be given to you; seek and you will find; knock and the door will be opened to you. For everyone who asks receives; he who seeks finds; and to him who knocks, the door will be opened. Which of you fathers, if your son asks for a fish, will give him a snake instead? Or if he asks for an egg, will give him a scorpion? If you then, though you are evil, know how to give good gifts to your children, how much more will your Father in heaven give the Holy Spirit to those who ask him!" (Luke 11:9-13)

There are, I have found, **three main hindrances** to people receiving the gift of the Holy Spirit:

Hindrance 1 - Doubt. "Yes, I can see it's a wonderful gift, but is it for me?"

Jesus tells us that God gives the Holy Spirit "to those who ask him." There is no discrimination with him. Factors of age, race or longevity in the Christian life do not matter. We have seen that Cornelius and his household received the Holy Spirit before Peter even stopped preaching his message. They can therefore only have been Christians for a few minutes (or even seconds) at the most!

When Peter was preaching on the Day of Pentecost he told his hearers that what they were seeing was the fulfilment of Joel's prophecy that God would pour out his Spirit on all people, young and old, male and female (Acts 2:17-18). Peter ends his sermon by telling the people that "The promise is for you and your children and for all who are far off—for all whom the Lord our God will call." (Acts 2:39)

It appears from the Bible that the only condition God attaches to receiving the Holy Spirit is that you have come to faith in the Lord Jesus Christ. As Peter says: "Repent and be baptised and you shall receive the gift of the Holy Spirit." (Acts 2:38)

Hindrance 2 - Inadequacy. "Am I good enough to receive the Holy Spirit?"

I have seen many sincere Christians labour under a misapprehension that they must somehow reach a certain level of holiness before they are able to receive the Holy Spirit. For them it's almost as if God sets a certain qualifying standard! They therefore spend much time praying and seeking to improve themselves, sometimes urged on by certain types of 'holiness' teaching, which emphasises repentance at the expense of grace.

Now while it is, of course, very right for Christians to seek holiness, it is wrong to see it as a 'qualification' for receiving the Holy Spirit. After all, how holy do we have to be? If we take God's perfect standards of holiness on board we can feel like we're trying to reach the moon by standing on a step ladder!

The truth is that we receive the gift of the Holy Spirit in exactly the same way as we receive salvation – by grace through faith. The wonderful fact is that by his death and resurrection, Jesus has made it possible for us to be completely righteous in God's sight by taking away our sin and giving us the gift of his own righteousness. As Paul tells us: "God made him [Jesus] who had no sin to be sin for us, so that in him we might become the righteousness of God." (2 Corinthians 5:21)

This happens the moment we believe. Through the merits of the shed blood of Christ we become perfectly righteous in the sight of God and therefore worthy, in Christ, to receive the Holy Spirit.

Hindrance 3 - Fear. "Will I get the right thing?"

In my years of ministry I have noticed that there is a natural fear of the unknown among the human race, especially when it comes to supernatural experiences like speaking in tongues. This is not helped by certain bogus stories that percolate in some Christian circles about people asking for the Holy Spirit and receiving 'the wrong thing'. However, in over 45 years of being a Christian I have never found a single one of these faith-destroying fables to be true!

The simple fact we can derive from Jesus' own teaching is that if we – as sinful, earthly beings – would not allow our own children to get the 'wrong thing' when they ask, how much more will our Father in heaven ensure we only get good things when we ask him for them.

Those 'good things' include the Holy Spirit. Just as we wouldn't give our children harmful things – stones, scorpions, snakes – when they ask for food, how much more will God ensure we receive only the pure goodness of the gift of the Holy Spirit when we come asking in faith.

How to Receive the Holy Spirit

7
How do we receive the Holy Spirit?

First remember the Holy Spirit is God's gift to you. A gift is something we cannot earn. There is nothing we can do to merit the gift which is entirely of God's grace. But encourage your faith by the realisation that, just as a father wants to give good gifts to his children, God wants to give you, his much loved child, the best gift of all – the gift of the Holy Spirit.

All that is needed for us to do is to set ourselves up to receive that gift. Here are some guidelines as to how we can be in a position to receive:

Step 1 – Eagerly desire.

Jesus said: "If anyone is thirsty, let him come to me and drink. Whoever believes in me, as the Scripture has said, streams of living water will flow from within him. By this he meant the Spirit, whom those who believed in him were later to receive." (John 7:37-38)

Jesus here is talking about the gift of the Holy Spirit which would be given to all believers. Note that he calls the Spirit 'living water' and continues the metaphor says that the Spirit will be given to all those who are thirsty.

We know that thirst is a fundamental desire of our human condition when the body is running short of fluids. I remember on a trip to Israel how our guide made sure we kept our water bottles filled up so we could quench our thirst that was generated by the intense heat of the climate.

Thirst is a condition of earnest desire. It is that sort of desire we need to be filled with the Holy Spirit. I remember the evening I received the Baptism in the Spirit; there may have been many things wrong with me but one thing that could not be faulted was my earnest desire for a new dimension in God that I knew the experience would bring.

Being thirsty, I simply came to God and drank in the 'water of life' that he poured out on me when I was prayed for. I not only 'drank' spiritually but also physically. The word for 'Spirit' in Hebrew (*ruach*) also means 'breath' and I believe that God fills us with his 'breath' as we breathe in the Spirit by faith.

When I pray for people to receive the Holy Spirit I tell them to do what Jesus commanded and "drink". Just as we drink a glass of water when we are thirsty, God wants us to drink in his Spirit by breathing him into our bodies. Yes, it's as easy as that!

Step 2 – Ask God.

Jesus told us: "Ask and it will be given to you; seek and you will find; knock and the door will be opened to you. For everyone who asks receives; he who seeks finds; and to him who knocks, the door will be opened." (Luke 11:9-10)

This is the promise of God from the lips of Jesus himself. Who can doubt that God will give us the Holy Spirit when we come to him in simple faith and ask?

Step 3 – Believe.

We have said the Holy Spirit is not received by our efforts, simply by believing the promises of God. Paul asks the Galatians: "Did you receive the Spirit by trying to obey the law or by receiving the word of God by faith?" (Gal 3:2)

Hence, as we are praying to receive the Holy Spirit let's believe that we are receiving! Remember that "faith comes by hearing and hearing the word of God" (Rom 10:17) so as you read the Bible, sit under anointed preaching or even read a book like this, God is filling your heart with faith to believe for the Holy Spirit.

Step 4 – Co-operate with the Holy Spirit.

Sometimes people so not realise that in order to speak in tongues we need to co-operate with the Holy Spirit. Hence they stand or sit with their mouths tightly shut expecting the Holy Spirit to speak in tongues through them.

However, if we look at what Acts 2:4 actually says: "And they [the disciples] were all filled with the Holy Spirit and they began to speak with other tongues, as the Spirit enabled them to do so."

Notice here that God did two things and the disciples did one: God filled them with the Holy Spirit and gave them the ability to speak in tongues. The disciples co-operated with the Spirit by speaking out the tongues as they were given the ability to do so.

Hence, when we are praying (or being prayed for) to receive the Holy Spirit, we need to realise that to complete the experience we actually have to speak in tongues ourselves. We need therefore to believe that God has filled us with the Spirit and move our mouth and tongue in faith and utter the words God is giving us. You might think at first they sound strange and even barbaric – well so do a lot of known languages. Don't let that put you off. Just speak out in faith!

It may also be that you only get a few words. There is no problem with this. After all, saying, "God is love!" in an unknown language is just as miraculous as reciting the complete book of Psalms in unknown tongues! And bear in mind that when a young child starts talking, they usually only utter a few words. But as they grow and practice speaking those few words soon become many. So also with our experience of speaking in tongues – as we practice speaking them on a daily basis more words will soon be added.

If we wish to grow in the gift of tongues (or any other gift, for that matter) we really need to heed the Lord's statement: "For whoever has will be given more, and they will have an abundance. Whoever does not have, even what they have will be taken from them." (Matt 25:29) In saying this the Lord was not advocating some heartless form of capitalism but rather urging us to develop the gifts God has given us. We all know that the natural gifts we have need to be used with diligence if they are to be developed. Hence, if I wish to be a good pianist, an Olympic athlete or a skilled engineer, I must learn to develop my gifts by practice, else I lose them. It is exactly the same with the gifts of the Spirit, including the gift of tongues. The more we 'practice' our tongues by speaking them regularly, the more the gift will grow in us. If we neglect the gift then we stand to lose it altogether.

Step 5 – Persevere.

Jesus tells us: seek and you will find. The word 'seek' is the present continuous and means "seek and keep on seeking." If we do not receive a full experience the first time we ask then we are encouraged to keep seeking God until we do. I have known quite a number of people who, although they haven't received when prayed for at the time, have none the less gone away and spoken in tongues on their own.

So if you are among those who have received prayer and nothing yet appears to have happened, be encouraged to continue to seek after the Holy Spirit, for Jesus himself assures us that everyone who seeks will find.

How to Receive the Holy Spirit

8
A Prayer for the Holy Spirit

If you are seeking the Baptism in the Holy Spirit and are not sure how to pray, here is a suggested prayer for the Holy Spirit:

"Heavenly Father, I thank you that through the blood of Jesus I am a child of God. I am now asking, as your child, for my rightful inheritance of being filled with the Holy Spirit. I believe the promise that this blessing is for everyone who you call, so I now ask you to fill me with the Holy Spirit. I believe and I receive. Thank-you Lord!"

How to Receive the Holy Spirit

A Final Word

Today, in many parts of the world, the church of Jesus Christ is growing faster than it's ever done in its history. The reason is that, in these 'last days', God is pouring out his Spirit "on all people" (Joel 2:28). This outpouring includes the Biblical experience of the Baptism in the Holy Spirit with speaking in tongues.

It is my prayer that this book has helped its readers in their seeking after this blessing from God. As you seek, remember the Holy Spirit is a gift from God, purchased with the blood of Jesus, and promised you as the first part of your spiritual inheritance while you are on the earth (Ephesians 1:14).

To repeat the words of Peter: "This promise is for you and your children and for all who are far off – for all whom the Lord our God will call." (Acts 2:39) Or as Jesus put it: "Seek and you will find!"

www.ingramcontent.com/pod-product-compliance
Lightning Source LLC
Chambersburg PA
CBHW072107290426
44110CB00014B/1858